Celebration of Hope

MARK LINK, S.J.

ThomasMore®
– An RCL Company –
Allen, Texas

IMPRIMI POTEST
Richard J. Baumann, S.J.

NIHIL OBSTAT
Rev. Msgr. Glenn D. Gardner, J.C.D.
Censor Librorum

IMPRIMATUR
† Most Rev. Charles V. Grahmann
Bishop of Dallas

June 28, 1999

The Nihil Obstat and Imprimatur are official declarations that the material reviewed is free of doctrinal or moral error. No implication is contained therein that those granting the Nihil Obstat and Imprimatur agree with the contents, opinions, or statements expressed.

ACKNOWLEDGMENT

Unless otherwise noted, all Scripture quotations are from Today's English Version text. Copyright © American Bible Society 1966, 1971, 1976, 1992. Used by permission.

COVER PHOTO: © Corbis / Digital Stock

INTERIOR PHOTOS: © Corbis / Digital Stock, © PhotoDisc, © Comstock, Inc.

Send all inquiries to:

Thomas More®
An RCL Company
200 East Bethany Drive
Allen, Texas 75002–3804

BOOKSTORES:
Call Bookworld Companies 888-444-2524 or fax 941-753-9396
PARISHES AND SCHOOLS:
Thomas More Publishing 800-822-6701 or fax 800–688–8356
INTERNATIONAL:
Fax Thomas More Publishing 972-264-3719

Visit our website at **www.rclweb.com**

Printed in the United States of America

Library of Congress Catalog Card Number: 99–74716

ISBN 0-88347-444-1

1 2 3 4 5 03 02 01 00 99

A Moment for Joy

They will become one flock
with one shepherd. JOHN 10:16

In the name of Jesus, the good shepherd,
I wish to make an appeal . . . to those
who for some reason or another are
separated from the practice of their faith.
On this eve of the Great Jubilee of the
2000th anniversary of the Incarnation,
Christ is seeking *you* out and inviting *you*
back to the community of faith.
Is this not the moment for *you* to experience
the joy of returning to the Father's house?
In some cases there may be obstacles
to eucharistic participation,
in some cases there may be memories
to be healed,
in all cases there is the assurance of
God's love and mercy.

JOHN PAUL II

Contents

Let us have a festival! Let us celebrate!

Jubilee 2000

Blow the trumpet . . .
Set the fiftieth year apart . . .
The whole year shall be sacred.

LEVITICUS 25:9–12

Jubilee celebrations to honor God
go back to ancient biblical times.
Jubilee 2000
continues this beautiful tradition.

And how better to honor God
than to celebrate the countless blessings
God has lavished upon us,
as a people and a nation.

So let us "blow the trumpet"
and keep festival with our God!

God has decided the number of the stars and calls each by name. Psalm 147:4

1 ✧ Celebrate Creation

How clearly the sky reveals God's glory!

PSALM 19:1

Author Arthur Gordon recalls how as a small boy he was awakened from sleep by his dad. Lifting him gently out of bed he carried him outside. The sky was ablaze with millions of stars. Pointing to the sky, his dad said "Look!" Suddenly, a star fell from the sky, leaving a trail of light behind it. Then another star fell; and another! "What's going on?" whispered the boy. "Shooting stars," said his father. For the next fifteen minutes father and son watched together in sacred silence. As they did, they were both transported into a world of beauty and mystery far beyond this one. It was a moment that neither would ever forget.

What was a memorable moment from my own childhood, especially involving a parent?

2 ✧ Tune in to Creation

I found him in the shining of the stars,
I marked him in the flowering of his field.

ALFRED LORD TENNYSON

I love to think of nature
as an unlimited broadcasting station,
through which God speaks to us
every hour, if we only will tune in.

GEORGE WASHINGTON CARVER

Two things fill my mind
with increasing wonder and awe—
the starry heavens above me
and the moral law within me.

IMMANUEL KANT

I saw the lightning's gleaming rod
Reach forth and write upon the sky
The awful autograph of God.

JOAQUIN MILLER

What aspect of God's broadcasting system fills me with wonder? What does it say to me about God?

3 ✧ Marvel at Creation

O LORD, our Lord,
your greatness is seen in all the world!

When I look at the sky,
which you have made,
at the moon and the stars
which you set in their places—

what are human beings,
that you made them,
mere mortals, that you care for them.

Yet you made them inferior
only to yourself; you crowned them
with glory and honor. . . .

O LORD, our Lord,
your greatness is seen in all the world!

PSALM 8:1–5, 9

What keeps me from seeing God's greatness in the world?

Poor eyes blur today's beauty;
Poor vision blurs tomorrow's possibilities.

4 ✧ Celebrate Vision

Where there is no vision,
the people perish. PROVERBS 29:18

One spring day, Carolyn Edwards drove her mother up a twisting mountain road. Suddenly, her mother saw what Carolyn brought her to see. As far as eye could see stretched a sea of red tulips, yellow daffodils, and purple hyacinths. She was speechless. "Who did this?" she gasped. A sign next to a small cottage explained: "What you see was done by one woman, one flower at a time, starting in 1958" "Think of it," her mother said, "One person with a vision turned drabness into beauty. It took forty years, but she did it." Imagine what I could do, if I had a vision and worked at it a little bit each day."

What is a vision that I still have concerning my life? What am I doing to make it a reality?

5 ✧ Claim the Vision

In the crimson light of a rising sun
fresh from the burning, creative hand of God,
I see great days ahead,
great days possible to men and women
of will and vision.

CARL SANDBURG

Vision is the Aladdin's lamp of the soul.
It is the divine spark
that lights the lamp of progress.
It is the hand that pushes aside the curtains
of night to let the sunrise in.

AMERICAN WAY

Only he who can see the invisible
can do the impossible.

FRANK GAINES

Do what you can, with what you have,
where you are.

THEODORE ROOSEVELT

I cannot change the world, but
I can change a part of the world.
What part might I change,
if I worked at it a little each day?

6 ✧ Live the Vision

In wild flights of fantasy,
I've streaked across the azure sky,
tunneled clouds, and touched the stars.

In daring flights of ecstasy
I've shed my shoes, walked on the wind,
and painted rainbows in the sky.

I've friended flights of birds,
hitched rides with eagles, and traveled
to worlds you've never dreamed of.

I've stowed away on meteors,
explored the Milky Way,
and planted my own flag on the moon.

Leaving behind my earthly skin,
I've skipped rope with lightning bolts,
danced with angels, and talked with God.

If I could talk with God what would I say? Well I can. What keeps me from saying it now?

Between tomorrow's dream and yesterday's regret is today's opportunity. E.C. McKenzie

7 ✧ Celebrate Dreams

God says,
"I will pour out my Spirit on everyone.
Your sons and daughters
will proclaim my message;
your young men will see visions,
and your old men will have dreams."

ACTS 2:17

"I have a dream that one day this nation will rise up and live out the true meaning of its creed: We hold these truths to be self-evident that all men are created equal.

"I have a dream that one day in the red hills of Georgia the sons of former slaves and the sons of former slave owners will be able to sit down together at the table of brotherhood. . . . This is our hope. This is our faith that I go back to the south with."

MARTIN LUTHER KING, JR.

How do a vision and a dream differ? What dream do I have?
What might I do to begin to make it a reality?

8 ✧ Believe the Dream

You see things; and you say "Why?"
But I dream things that never were;
and I say "Why not?"

GEORGE BERNARD SHAW

It's not tragic to die with an unfulfilled dream;
it's tragic not to dream.

ANONYMOUS

Most look up and admire the stars.
A champion climbs a mountain
and grabs one.

H. JACKSON BROWN, JR.

The future belongs to those who
believe in the beauty of their dreams.

ELEANOR ROOSEVELT

When you dream alone, it stays a dream,
but when you dream with others,
it can become a reality.

KAHLIL GIBRAN

*What dream do I have
for the Church? The nations?
How might I work with
others to make it a reality?*

9 ✧ Do the Dream

The one who misses all the fun
Is he who says, "It can't be done."
In solemn pride he stands aloof,
And greets each venture with reproof.

Had he the power he'd efface,
The history of the human race.
We'd have no radio or motor cars,
No street lit by electric stars;

No telegraph nor telephone,
We'd linger in the age of stone.
The world would sleep if things were run
By men who say, "It can't be done."

ANONYMOUS

Vision without work is a dream.
Work without vision is drudgery.
Vision and work together
make the dream a reality.

What are some reasons why dreams die stillborn?

Earth with her thousand voices praises God.

Samuel Taylor Coleridge

10 ✧ Celebrate the Father

God spoke to our ancestors . . . through the prophets,
but in these last days
God has spoken to us through his Son.

HEBREWS 1:1–2

God spoke to us through three words. The first was the cosmic word: creation. Just as the beauty of a song tells us something of its writer, the beauty of creation tells us something of its Creator.

The second word was the inspired word. God spoke it mainly by deeds; that is, God did not just say, "Israel, I love you." God showed it through loving actions.

The third word is the incarnate word. Jesus is the incarnate word; he is the "word of God made flesh." Jesus is God's final word. "Whoever has seen me," said Jesus, "has seen the Father."

JOHN 14:9

How might we help people today hear and respond better to God's word?

11 ✧ Embrace the Father

God does not love us for what we are,
but we are because God loves us.

PETER VAN BREEMAN

To fall in love with God
is the greatest of all romances;
to seek God,
the greatest of all adventures;
to find God
the greatest of all human achievements.

RAPHAEL SIMON

Why do you close your eyes to see God?
See him with your eyes open—
in the form of the poor, the starved,
the illiterate, and the afflicted.

AUTHOR UNKNOWN

It is the heart that experiences God,
not the reason.

BLAISE PASCAL

When and how have I experienced God's presence and help on some occasion?

12 ✧ Praise the Father

I sing the mighty power of God
that made the mountains rise;
That spread the flowing seas abroad,
And built the lofty skies. . . .

Lord, how your wonders are displayed,
Where e'er I turn my eye:
If I survey the ground I tread,
Or gaze upon the sky!

There's not a plant or flower below,
But makes your glories known;
And clouds arise, and tempests blow,
By order from your throne;

While all that borrows life from you
Is ever in your care,
And everywhere that man can be,
Thou, God, are present there.

ISAAC WATTS

Can I recall a time when God's presence in nature moved me deeply?

It wasn't the nails that held Jesus on the cross,
but his love for us. Anonymous

13 ✧ Celebrate the Son

The Word became a human being.

JOHN 1:14

The world in which the Son of God was born was a cruel world. Men were sold on the auction block to die for the entertainment of others.

It was a pain-filled world. The lame and the blind were taken for granted, like stormy weather and earthquakes.

It was an ugly world. The poor and the weak were pawns of the rich and the powerful.

Into this world, Jesus was born, not as a lofty prince, safe from its evils, but as a lowly peasant, vulnerable to all of them.

Which person of the Trinity do I find it easiest or hardest to relate to? Why do I find it hard or easy to relate to Jesus?

14 ✧ Learn from the Son

Jesus came not to eradicate suffering,
but to fill it with his presence.

PAUL CLAUDEL

Jesus is the way to the Father,
the truth about the Father,
and the life of the Father.

ANONYMOUS

Jesus' power working in us
is able to do so much more
than we can ask for,
or even think of.

EPHESIANS 3:20

How can I ever creep
after I've felt the urge to fly.

ANONYMOUS

Why not let Jesus take over my life? He can do more with it than I can.

ANONYMOUS

What are some reasons why I hesitate to let Jesus take over my life?

15 ✧ Believe the Son

Jesus,
I believe you entered our world of hate,
that we might enter your world of love.

Jesus,
I believe you are always with us,
even though we are not always with you.

Jesus,
I believe you reached out to us,
that we might reach out to others.

Jesus,
I believe you understand us,
even if we don't understand ourselves.

Jesus,
I believe you are truly God's son,
because you've treated us as your own.

Why do I believe in Jesus?
Why does Jesus believe in me?

Surely you know that you are God's temple
and that God's Spirit lives in you! 1 Corinthians 3:16

16 ✧ Celebrate the Spirit

Jesus said to his disciples . . .
"Peace be with you . . .
Receive the Holy Spirit."

JOHN 20:22

Without the Spirit, God is far away in some unknown realm; and the cosmos is wrapped in mystery. Without the Spirit, Jesus is just a teacher who lived long ago; and Scripture is just a dusty book. Without the Spirit, the Church is an outdated social club.

In the Spirit, God is present in the midst of our world; and the cosmos is birthing the kingdom. In the Spirit, Jesus is the firstborn of the new creation; and Scripture is the living Word of God. In the Spirit, the Church is God's people on their way to the new Jerusalem.

How have I experienced the presence of the Spirit in my life?

17 ✧ *Live in the Spirit*

To distance ourselves from sin
is not enough; we must live in the Spirit.
Who lives in the Spirit is showered
with blessings. Love leads the shower.
the others are simply glorious colors
in love's rainbow.

GALATIANS 5:22

Love is God giving us life.
Joy is love singing in the heart.
Peace is love trusting in God.
Patience is love willing to wait.
Kindness is love smiling and inviting.
Generosity is love giving itself away.
Faithfulness is love never growing weary.
Gentleness is love melting hearts.
Self-control is love staying in shape.

When my spirit soars,
my body falls on its knees.

GEORG CHRISTOPH LICTENBERG

Which three blessings above
do I need most right now? Why?

18 ✧ Call upon the Spirit

Breathe into me, Spirit of God,
that I may think what is holy.

Drive me, Spirit of God,
that I may do what is holy.

Draw me, Spirit of God,
that I may love what is holy.

Strengthen me, Spirit of God,
that I may preserve what is holy.

Guide me, Spirit of God,
that I may never lose what is holy.

SAINT AUGUSTINE

Holy Spirit, Paraclete,
perfect in us the work begun by Jesus.

POPE JOHN XXIII

Traditionally, Christians have prayed to the Spirit for light and strength. Why do I need light and strength?

Your word is a lamp to guide me
and a light for my path. Psalm 119:105

19 ✧ Celebrate Scripture

All Scripture is inspired by God
and is useful for teaching the truth,
rebuking error, correcting faults,
and giving instruction for right living.

2 TIMOTHY 3:16

In To Kill a Mockingbird, Atticus Finch says to his children, "The only way to understand people is to crawl inside their skins, see what they see, hear what they hear, feel what they feel."

The same is true God's inspired word, Scripture. Studying it and discussing it is not enough. We must break open God's inspired word, crawl inside it, press it to our heart, savor its sweetness, and relate it to our everyday life, and share it with others.

What keeps me from breaking open God's word and savoring and sharing it?

20 ✧ Lay Hold of Scripture

I read the Bible to know what people
ought to do, and I read the newspaper
to know what they are doing.

JOHN HENRY NEWMAN

Lay hold of the Bible
until it lays hold of you.

WILLIAM H. HOUGHTON

In the Old Testament
the New Testament lies concealed;
in the New Testament,
the Old Testament lies revealed.

ST. AUGUSTINE

Radio is like the Old Testament;
you hear God's Word.
Television is like the New Testament;
you not only hear God's Word,
but also see it come alive in Jesus.

INSPIRED BY FULTON SHEEN

*In what sense does
the New Testament
lie concealed in the Old?*

21 ✧ Break Open Scripture

Lord Jesus, look upon us with love,
especially those of us who have left you
behind in some Good Friday tomb.

Surprise us on the road
and walk along with us,
as you did with the two disciples
going to Emmaus.
Break open the Scriptures for us,
as you did for them.

Come into our house
and dine with us,
as you did with them.
Take into your hands our bread;
bless it, break it, and share it.

Heal us of our spiritual blindness,
as you healed their blindness,
that we, too, might recognize you
in all your risen glory.

How are the breaking of
the word and bread related?

If the Church is to remain on its feet,
it must get on its knees.

22 ✧ Celebrate the Church

Jesus is the head of his body, the Church;
he is the source of the body's life.

COLOSSIANS 1:18

Before his conversion, Paul was going from Jerusalem to Damascus to arrest Christians. Suddenly a light flashed around him. "He fell to the ground and heard a voice say, 'Saul, Saul! Why do you persecute me?' 'Who are you, Lord?' he asked, 'I am Jesus, whom you persecute,' the voice said."

ACTS 9:4-5

Paul was baffled. He wasn't persecuting Jesus—only his followers. Then it hit him like another bolt of lightning: Jesus and his followers form one body. He wrote later to the Christians of Rome, "We are one body in union with Christ."

ROMANS 12:5

What keeps me from seeing the Church more clearly as the Body of the Risen Christ?

23 ✧ Be the Church

A reporter asked Mother Teresa,
"What's wrong with the Church today?"
Mother Teresa responded, "You and I.
We are what's wrong with the Church.
We are the Church."

If we find a perfect church, join it!
Then it will no longer be perfect.

BILLY GRAHAM

A floundering world in a helpless mess,
needs the Church at its very best.

ANONYMOUS

We can't have God for a Father,
if we don't have the Church for a mother.

SAINT AUGUSTINE

Put yourself at the disposal of
the Church. . . . It needs you. . . .
You are its future.

POPE JOHN PAUL II TO SWISS YOUTH

What keeps me from putting myself more fully at the Church's disposal?

24 ✧ Embrace the Church

I think I shall never see
a Church that's all it ought to be:
A Church whose members never stray
beyond the straight and narrow way.
A Church that has no empty pews,
whose pastor never has the blues. . . .

Such perfect churches there may be,
but none of them are known to me.
But still, we'll work and pray and plan
to make our own the best we can.

AUTHOR UNKNOWN

The Church is both divine and human.
It is a blend of light and darkness.
It radiates just enough light
for those who want to see
and just enough darkness
for those whose disposition is
otherwise.

YVES CONGAR: ADAPTED

*What are some ways I might
participate more fully
in building up the Church?*

You are a child of God.
Please call home. Bumper Sticker

25 ✧ Celebrate Prayer

The disciples said to Jesus,
"Lord teach us to pray."

LUKE 11:1

A friend went to visit artist Henri Matisse. When the friend arrived at his home, his nerves were frayed and he was exhausted. Matisse said to him, "My dear friend, you must find the artichokes in your life." Then Matisse took him out to his garden. When they came to a patch of artichokes, Matisse stopped and said, "Every morning after working a while, I come here, sit, and just remain very still, looking at the artichokes. I always find new combinations of color and fantastic patterns. No one is allowed to disturb me in this ritual. . . . It gives me fresh inspiration, necessary relaxation, and a new perspective toward my work."

When, where and how do I usually pray daily?

26 ✧ *Turn to Prayer*

If I'm to busy to pray, I'm too busy.

E.C. MCKENZIE

Whoever has lost contact with God
lives on the same dead-end street
as the person who denies God.

MILTON MARCY

Life is fragile—handle with prayer.

E.C. MCKENZIE

Prayer is exhaling the spirit of man
and inhaling the spirit of God.

EDWIN KIETH

"In prayer, the important thing is not
to think much but to love much."

THERESA OF AVILA

Oh, help me, Lord, to take the time
To set all else aside,
That in the secret place of prayer
I may with you abide.

AUTHOR UNKNOWN

What are some aids to prayer that I find helpful?

27 ✧ Cherish Prayer

I pray because I am a Christian,
and to do what a Christian must do,
I need strength.

I pray because there's confusion in my life,
and to know what is right,
I need light.

I pray because I have questions,
and to keep growing in the faith,
I need help.

I pray because most of what I have
has been given to me,
and I ought to give thanks.

I pray because Jesus prayed,
and if he considered it important,
so should I.

Which of the above reasons apply to me especially?

No Christian escapes a taste of wilderness
on the way to the promised land. Evelyn Underhill

28 ✧ Celebrate the Cross

"When you pass through deep waters,
I will be with you; your troubles
will not overwhelm you."

ISAIAH 43:1–2

"How often we look upon God as our last and feeblest resource. We go to God because we have nowhere else to go. And then we learn that the storms of life have driven us not upon the rocks but into the desired haven."

GEORGE MACDONALD

What might God's reason be?

"Not until each loom is silent
And the shuttles cease to fly,
Will God unroll the pattern
And explain the reason why
The dark threads are as needful
In the weaver's skillful hand
As the threads of gold and silver
For the pattern which is
planned."

AUTHOR UNKNOWN

29 ✧ Carry the Cross

When things go wrong,
as they sometimes will,
When the road you're trudging
seems all uphill . . .
When care is pressing you down a bit,
Rest, if you must—but don't you quit.

AUTHOR UNKNOWN

For every hill I've had to climb . . .
For all the blood and sweat and grime . . .
My heart sings but a grateful song—
These were things that made me strong.

ANONYMOUS

All which I took from thee
I did but take not for thy harms,
But just that thou might'st seek it
in my arms.

FRANCIS THOMPSON

Recall a time in your life
when a cross turned out
to be a blessing in disguise.

30 ✧ Trust the Cross

For ev'ry pain we must bear.
For ev'ry burden, ev'ry care,
there's a reason.

For ev'ry grief that bows the head,
for ev'ry teardrop that is shed,
there's a reason.

For ev'ry hurt, for ev'ry plight,
For ev'ry lonely, pain-racked night,
there's a reason.

But if we trust God, as we should,
It will work out for our good.
He knows the reason.

AUTHOR UNKNOWN

Who never ate bread in sorrow,
Who never spent the darksome hours
Weeping and watching for the morrow
He knows you not, you heavenly
Powers.

JOHANN WOLFGANG VON GOETHE

Why do I agree with the unknown author? Or with Von Goethe? Why don't I?

Friends are a second existence. Joseph Roux

31 ✧ Celebrate Friends

Jesus said, "I call you friends."

JOHN 15:15

We are all travelers in the wilderness of the world, and the best we can find in our travels is an honest friend. He is a fortunate voyager who finds many. They keep us worthy of ourselves.

ROBERT LOUIS STEVENSON

We force no doors in friendship, but like the Christ in Revelation, we stand reverently at the door without to knock. . . . The glory of friendship is not the outstretched hand, nor the kindly smile . . . it is the spiritual inspiration that comes to one when he discovers that someone else believes in him and is willing to trust him. My friends have come unsought. The great God gave them to me.

RALPH WALDO EMERSON

Why must spouses become close friends before becoming committed lovers?

32 ✧ Know Friends

When the talk is easy,
and the feeling is warm;
When the memories are many,
and the time is too short;
then I know I'm with a true friend.

ANONYMOUS

A true friend is someone
who dances with me in the sunlight
and walks beside me in the shadows.

ANONYMOUS

God's finger touches my life
when I make a true friend.

INSPIRED BY MARY DAWSON HUGHES

A true friend knows who I am,
understands where I've been,
accepts who I've become,
and still gently invites me to grow.

AUTHOR UNKNOWN

*How do I invite
a close friend to grow?*

33 ✧ Bless Friends

May there always be work
for your hand to do.

May your purse
always hold a coin or two.

May the sun always shine
on your windowpane.

May a rainbow
be certain to follow each rain.

May the hand of a friend
always be near you.

May God fill your heart
with gladness to cheer you.

OLD IRISH BLESSING

I love you more for what
I am when I am with you
than for what you are.
Do I agree? Why? Why not?

People who shine from the inside
look twenty years younger. Dolly Parton

34 ✧ Celebrate Maturity

Now that I am old and my hair is gray,
do not abandon me.

PSALM 71:18

"The number of senior citizens presents the nation with increased opportunities: the opportunity to draw upon their skill. . . . It is not enough for a great nation to have added new years to life—our objective must be to add new life to those years."

JOHN F. KENNEDY

What are some ways to achieve the objective that Kennedy cites above?

Goethe finished Faust at 81. Tennyson wrote Crossing the Bar at 83. Verdi composed Othello at 84. Titian painted his Last Supper at 99. Experts say if we keep mentally alert, we can be as productive at 80 as we are at 20. Creativity isn't touched by age; and judgment and reason are often better.

35 ✧ Embrace Maturity

Grandmother started walking
five miles a day when she was 60.
She's 95 now, and we don't know
where the heck she is.

ELLEN DEGENERIS

Retirement at 65, ridiculous. When
I was 65, I still had pimples.

GEORGE BURNS

A person doesn't become old until
his regrets take the place of his dreams.

JOHN R. NOE

I don't know what the big deal is about
age. People who shine from the inside
look twenty years younger.

DOLLY PARTON

Expect the best! It lies not in the past.
God ever keeps the good wine till last!

WILLIAM PIERSON MERRILL

Do I believe the latter years of life can be among the best years? Why? Why not?

36 ✧ Prize Maturity

"Dear God:
Why do you let people grow old?
Signed: Conroy"
"Dear Conroy:
I often find the way you think
quite puzzling.
For me,
the most beautiful moment on earth
is old people.
They are my human sunsets.
Signed: God."

JOHN R. POWERS

LORD God . . . I have relied on you . . .
since the day I was born. . . .
My life has been an example to many,
because you have been
my strong defender. . . .
There is no one like you.

PSALM 71: 5–7, 19

*If God intended maturity
to be a beautiful moment,
what might we do to
insure that it will be?*

Ask not what your country can do for you;
ask what you can do for your country. John F. Kennedy

37 ✧ Celebrate America

Freedom is what we have . . .
Stand then as free people.

GALATIANS 5:1

I was born on July 4, 1776, and the Declaration of Independence is my birth certificate. . . . I am the nation. . . . I am Lee and Grant and Abe Lincoln. . . . When freedom called I answered. . . . I left my heroic dead in Flanders Fields, on the rock of Corregidor, on the bleak slopes of Korea, and in the steaming jungle of Vietnam. . . . I am quiet villages—and cities that never sleep. . . . I am 330,000 churches where my people worship God as they think best. . . . I am the nation . . . and, God willing, in freedom I will . . . remain a citadel to freedom and a beacon of hope to the world.

OTTO WHITTAKER

What concerns do I have for America? What signs of hope do I see?

38 ✧ Work for America

We have grown in numbers, wealth
and power, as no other nation has. . . .
But we have . . . forgotten the gracious
hand which preserved us.

ABRAHAM LINCOLN

The righteousness of our cause
must always underlie our strength.
For as was written long ago:
"Unless the LORD guard the city,
in vain does the guard keep watch."

JOHN F. KENNEDY

With a good conscience
our only sure reward,
with history the final judge of our deeds,
let us go forth to lead the land we love,
asking his blessing and his help,
but knowing that here on earth
God's work must truly be our own.

JOHN F. KENNEDY

What am I doing for America? What might I do?

39 ✧ Pray for America

I sought for the . . . greatness of America . . .
in her fertile fields and boundless forests—
and it was not there. . . .

[I sought for it] in her rich mines and
her vast world commerce—
and it was not there. . . .

[I sought for it] in her democratic Congress
and matchless Constitution—
and it was not there.

Not until I went into the churches
of America . . . did I understand
the secret of her genius and power.

America is great because she is good,
but if America ever ceases to be good
she will cease to be great.

ALEXIS DE TOCQUEVILLE

*What signs of goodness
do I still see in America?*

When love touches the heart
the sweet bird of hope joins the party.

LORD . . .
I will always put my hope in you;
I will praise you more and more.

PSALM 71:14

Ben Carson grew up in poverty. His mother suffered a divorce when he was only eight. She worked at two and sometimes three low-paying jobs to give her two sons a better life. She also encouraged them. "You can be anything you want to be. Just ask God. He will help you, if you help yourself."

Today, Dr. Carson is one of America's top pediatric neurosurgeons. Speaking to high schoolers at his old alma mater, he said, "Think big! Set your sights as high as Mount Everest. Nobody was born to be a failure."

CHRISTOPHER NEWS NOTES

What are some things on which I have set my sights?

41 ✧ Be Filled with Hope

Great hopes make great men.

THOMAS FULLER

Hope sees the invisible
and achieves the impossible.

AUTHOR UNKNOWN

A baby is God's opinion
that the world should go on.

CARL SANDBURG

Let us be like a bird
for a moment perched
on a frail branch while he sings;
Though he feels it bend,
yet he sings his song,
knowing that he has wings.

VICTOR HUGO

Our greatest songs are still unsung.

HUBERT H. HUMPHREY

What are some songs
that are still unsung?

42 ✧ Christ Is Our Hope

[Faith] is the mother of dreams.
Over the gray world,
ruined by deluge and death,
it has sought ever and found
the arching rainbow of hope.

ALBERT HAYDON

The resurrection
of Jesus Christ is our hope today.
It is our assurance
that we have a living Savior
to help us live as we should.

And in the end, when we set forth
on that last great journey,
we shall not travel an uncharted course,
but we will go on a planned voyage—
from life to death to eternal life.

RAYMOND MACKENDREE

*In what sense is life
without Christ a hopeless
end and life with Christ
an endless hope?*